GUARACARA

Fawzia Muradali Kane is an architect and poet. Born in San Fernando, Trinidad and Tobago, she came to the UK on a scholarship to study architecture. She now lives in London and is a director of KMK Architects. Her debut poetry collection *Tantie Diablesse* (Waterloo Press 2011) was longlisted for the 2012 OCM Bocas Prize for Caribbean Literature. In 2014, Thamesis Publications produced her long sequence *Houses of the Dead* as an illustrated pamphlet. Her short story 'Anguilla City' was the 2018 City of Stories winner for Westminster in London. Her prose poem 'Eric' won second prize in 2023's National Poetry Competition.

GUARACARA

FAWZIA MURADALI KANE

CARCANET POETRY

First published in Great Britain in 2025 by
Carcanet
Main Library, The University of Manchester
Oxford Road, Manchester, M13 9PP
www.carcanet.co.uk

A CIP catalogue record for this book is
available from the British Library.

ISBN 978 1 80017 487 0

Book design by Andrew Latimer, Carcanet
Typesetting by LiteBook Prepress Services
Printed in Great Britain by SRP Ltd, Exeter, Devon

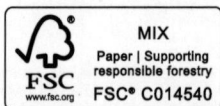

MIX
Paper | Supporting
responsible forestry
FSC
www.fsc.org   FSC® C014540

The publisher acknowledges financial
assistance from Arts Council England.

Supported using public funding by
ARTS COUNCIL
ENGLAND

CONTENTS

GUARACARA

LET US MOURN THE DEATH OF KING SUGAR

ANCESTRAL CODA

GUARACARA

I AM LOSING MY EYESIGHT &

this street grime & coughs of muffler
smoke begin to blossom into a blast

of potted anthuriums, while parakeets strobe
their flash-wings & chitter on wires above –

if a thing does not move, is it still alive?
This rainy season plays me, makes me huddle

under its thump beat on a galvanised tin porch
roof, the tinkle of someone's piano lessons.

Corbeaux hover while notes slide down Mon Repos
pavements & I am learning a different language,

how to grasp new signals: fading sunlight that sculpts
wall against shadow, a hissing cat gliding ahead as guide,

or the hairs of my skin, rising at the sound of footsteps
on stairs, & the slowness of a curtain being drawn.

GUARACARA

1

Just before the polio epidemic closed the islands down, my uncle gave me a morocoy. At least it was alive. The last time he went hunting in the rainforest, he came back with a squirrel's tail, and he couldn't understand why I was so upset. *But look how fluffy*, he said. It wasn't. It was threadbare. Pictures of squirrels in Foreign show them bushy and red. Trini squirrels maaga for so, despite their greediness. Years later, I learnt that hunters were paid a bounty per squirrel, as they loved to chew through the hard skin of coffee and cocoa pods for the sweet beans inside.

2

Guaracara river was a black thing, iridescent, slow moving, sticky with waste from the refinery as it poured its pollution into the Gulf of Paria. The banks were slick with oil. The trees were stick-thin, stained outlines of a cartoon hell. Nothing could grow there.

3

There used to be a railway line, snaking behind these back streets of Marabella. It ran a few hundred yards to the north of our house, past the empty plots stretching under the huge spread of the ancient samaan tree behind us, and over a Bailey bridge spanning the river. I remember the freight trains, trundling past with wagons heavy with fresh-cut cane stalks. A sickly molasses scent wafted well after they passed. My brother warned us off going too close. He said once a boy tried to grab a cane stalk while the train was moving, and had his arm pulled off.

4

Ramnanan, Ramsamooj, Pariag, Sooknanan, Thackorie: streets to play in, to fetch your brother's cricket balls when he hit a six, or ride chopper bikes bumping over potholes in the narrow roads. My friend's father built a dollyhouse under their house. Her older sisters were so elegant, wearing makeup while cooking and cleaning in their mini skirts and shindig shoes.

5

After its life as a sugar distribution centre ended, Marabella town became a satellite of Texaco refinery, where workers settled with their families. Shops and worker's eating places stretched along its main road. But when the wind blew down this way, towards the residential districts, the air would stink of sulphur and choked us when we breathed, scratched the back of our throats while we played in the streets. The corrosive rain rotted the galvanise roofs to holes and powdery rust.

6

There was a man who owned land at the street dead-end, near the railway bank. He had set out an orchard years before- mangoes, pomerac, sour cherries. Guavas, downs and pawpaw grew semi-wild along the edges, bird-shit sown. On the Sunday after he sold the land, he poured boiling water over the tree trunks and roots, so no one else could pick the fruit.

7

At seven o clock, noon, and 4 o clock, the Whistle went off in the refinery to signal the start and end of the working day. If we heard it while walking to school, we knew we were late. It was a remnant of the war days, an air-raid siren for the refinery, which provided fuel for the motherland of Empire.

8

Every morning the man across the road, who prided himself as a very knowledgeable and religious man, would line up his six sons in their house, according to their age, and flog them. The smallest first. He would leave the oldest two for last. They were the tallest boys in these parts, known for being strong as bullocks but not worth schooling. If my uncle visited us during these times, he would peer through our window and shout *daily blessing bwai!* and the man would stop. Two years later the religious man emigrated with his family to Foreign. The youngest boy married a delicate young woman, and kept her captive for months. Her uncle somehow managed to retrieve her, and brought her back home.

9

The train system was broken up and buses took over the roads. The rails and wood sleepers remained. We played in the gaps between overgrown razor grass. My oldest sister would carry me for walks, cradled on her shoulder, pretending she was grown up. Once she tripped on a stone. I was thrown over the rails, landed on my face onto the gravel bank. I didn't cry. My mother told me how she slapped my sister after seeing my bloodied face. I don't remember this, but my nose is crooked.

10

Once a centipede stung a boy. His leg swelled like a purple boot. *Santipee nearly kill'im!* His family went to live in Canada. He died driving on the icy roads there, many decades later.

11

Over the years, squatters settled over the rusting rails, along the unclaimed state land. They built dwellings from discarded timber, cardboard and recycled plywood – materials easy to dismantle and reassemble quickly, should the government bulldozers turn up unannounced. In time, the area became known as the Line.

12

My sister would complain that I never cried. Her friends' toddler siblings liked to bawl. Why wasn't I like them, chubby and noisy? She solved this by locking me in the wardrobe. When I was put in, the dark was so thick you could touch it. She would always relent, open the door, scoop me up with a guilty hug, but sometimes I fainted before. I knew the strange sleep was coming when the whine of the mosquitoes crescendo-ed to sirens. I remember my sister being beaten by my mother with a length of orange peel, but I cannot say if this was the reason.

13

We would hear the adults whispering about polio in the news. While playing with the other children near the Line, someone said a whole family in the countryside got sick after eating one of their pigs on their farm. Another said it started in Mayaro near the sea, and was travelling to the towns. Travelling. Our word for taking taxis. Flag them down with a pointing finger. Climb onto the seat, join the other passengers. The disease became a live thing. It expanded and billowed dark like the refinery flambeaux, moved with a will of its own.

14

Pappy came home with a truckload of scrap iron and chains. A couple of his refinery welder friends were sitting on the tray. By sunset the swing was finished. My sister and I drive past the old house sometimes. The swing is still there, standing in the immaculate garden of the house's new owners.

15

The time came when we couldn't walk into each other's houses or play in the street. That epidemic year the Common Entrance exam was delayed. The newspapers began to publish mock exam questions, while the School Teachers Association tried to give lessons over the radio. Pappy went to school to collect my homework. I could tell he was enjoying this more than me. An assignment was to guess the number of grass leaves on our lawn. He went into his shed and came back with a ball of string, a mallet and wooden pegs. My heart sank. He pegged out the small front garden, tying the string into foot-wide grids. Mister Morocoy kept me company, eating the scuffed patches of lawn under the swing, while I counted. Pappy handed in the pages of methodology, calculations and conclusion. Mrs. Murchie called me on the phone. She laughed, *you were supposed to guess, that's all.*

16

I remember when the river caught fire. The water was already thickened with oil-sludge. Someone lit their rubbish and the wind threw sparks onto the water's surface. We stood in our street a half-mile away, and watched the bonfire's flames grow taller than the houses. It burnt through the night, despite the drizzle. The glow moved slowly, followed the river's slackened flow to the sea, catching the crude covered trees along the banks, to bring death to the already dead.

17

We queued up with the Marabella Line children for the vaccination in a temporarily opened school: dosed with a sugar cube on a plastic spoon, smothered in pink syrup. A girl behind me bawled non-stop. Pappy was silent on the way home. Later that day he brought us ice cream and fried wontons. I put Mister Morocoy out on the lawn, went inside for ice cream. When I returned, it had disappeared. We searched everywhere, even the guppy filled drains that lined the road outside. I cried for days.

PRAISE TO THE INVISIBLES
for Antoinette Pieterson & Darnella Frazier

'This is the time for Big Poems, roaring up out of sleaze, poems from ice, from vomit, and from tainted blood...'
                                                    Gwendolyn Brooks

Big Poems have broad shoulders, pulled back for the pivot and unleash of the punch. Their hands clap around ropes, pull down the hollows of bronze. Their decibels rise higher than the keen of sirens, beyond thresholds of pain no human can bear, as a sister weeps when she runs alongside the man who is carrying her brother's limp body – oh! how that image played out then, and still plays out now, with children who forget too easily and keep playing: they laugh then stop, hide then stop, buy skittles.   Stop.

While pavements crack with fallen helmets and shattered skulls, and drums are beaten with stolen batons, among that chorus of lion roars let us anoint the others too:

the empty fisted, the small-voiced, holders of quietude, termitous and fungal decomposers of white noise. They have their own work. Hush. Listen. They are scratching, chipping away to unsettle and undermine foundations, dismantle intricate scaffolds that shored up structures, suffocating so many, for too long. Their words resonate through the earth's surface, undulating to a force until all implodes. They will prime the world for renewal, ready for the harrow of heavyweights.

ANIMITA

There is death here. I can smell it.
　　　　Will no one care to stop?　　　　The flowers
　　　　　　　　　　have dried while still tied to their stakes.

　　　　The doors to the casa have fallen off
the furniture has been stolen.　A ghost
　　　　　　　　　　bicycle leans against my small cross.

Pray for her　　　　is painted on its white frame.
Sometimes　　　I find remnants of candles
flecks of ash

　　　　and spent wax dotted
　　　　　　　　on the ground's dry dust. Sometimes

I dream of my mother's laughter
　　　　while she washes my hair, pours
　　　　　　　　a tin of water over my skin.　　　　I want
　　　　　　　　　　to fall asleep against the sound of rain.

*Animitas are roadside shrines in Latin America, where someone
has died suddenly, usually a traffic accident.*

THE MAHOGANY COPSE

In this thin air they show us their own ghosts.
They ignore the time of wounds, and falling.

There are no tales of shaven skin, or limbs
pulled apart and cut to be burnt, as they know

the wicking of blood has its own grain. But soon,
they will group to form a timepiece of our seasons,

which will slide under our bodies, and blend
their ichor tint with ash, while we sleep.

When you stood looking out at the sky from the sea's edge, did the sand mould itself around your feet? Did hunger lift you, push you towards the forest? Did the trees speak to you of giants? Did they show you the path already worn to hard clay through the undergrowth? Did they show you how to suckle your young, or which herbs were bitter medicine? Did you learn how to read the light on the grasslands and the shadows under woodland leaves? Did you strip the clothing off the Mother? Did you form mud to brick? Did you build higher? Did you teach how to kill for love or for hate? Did you feel the ground at your feet harden to concrete? Did you notice how the road glows with an oily sheen, how its edges flicker with a blue flame that has set the world alight? Despite the barren beyond, did you keep to the path? Did you see ahead, or did the burning anthracite cloud your vision?

THE BULL FELL
after Mahmoud Darwish

'...*birds hovered above/ the hem of the place, and exchanged some symbols.*'
The Cypress Broke, Mahmoud Darwish (tr. Fady Joudah)

The bull fell like a tree, with red sap pouring on
the earth of the arena, dark wine pooling under swags of velvet, green
as sea-moss that draped the brass band's stage. No one got hurt.
        The vehicles
sped behind the bleachers, towards the butchers' stalls, where dust
        blew
into tarpaulin screens that hid sawdust and knives.../ The bull fell, but
the team of black mules tried to stand still, so their harness wouldn't
        change
its position. They nodded feathered heads and stamped hooves above
the arena's wooden edge, impatient to flick the hem of el presidente's
        symbol
and drag away their payload of death. A woman remembered last
        week's storm,
she covered her head when the wind whipped up the dust again.../
        And the bull
fell. And the band continued playing while el presidente said:
*maybe this bull deserves to be freed, to go back to fields where he can grow
        old*
with his bloodline around him, waiting their turn to enter village arenas.
        But few
in this crowd agreed, for a matador must kill quick and clean in front
        of his lovers.
And a boy said: *I must practice passing the cape perfectly.*
It isn't as easy as it looks. And a girl said: *After all this, perhaps today*
is when I will learn to face the charge, because this bull fell.

And a young banderillero said: *Perhaps my battles are now complete because I helped to fell the bull.* And I said
to myself in this moment of clarity:
the bull fell, sword through spine, his death was nothing at all.
There was no meaning to his suffering: the bull fell!

NAMESAKE
i.m. Fawzia of Egypt
(5.11.1921 – 2.7.2013)

I am not the daughter of a king, or even the sister of one. I was not
given as a contract between countries, to add stature to bandits.

I know the grief of homesickness. My uncle loved me, as yours did,
when he saved your *whisper of a body*, and took you home.

You bartered with your daughter's life. I have nothing for such
an exchange. You discovered that to learn to love is to live. I had that too.

When your sisters fled, you chose to stay with your new love, became
    a stranger
in your own land. There are too many dangers if we remain ourselves.

And if my love also dies before I grow old, where will I walk? Will all
we have built fade into pictures, where we stand sad-faced and silent?

Beyond the decay of shrouds and caskets, lies the grace of caged lives.
May our passing be quick, our bodies washed by women who cry,

the courtyard swept before pallbearers jostle, the muezzin hushed among
all emptiness that remains. Let these be deaths that give light to wonder!

EVE PREPARES THE MEAL IN THE GARDEN

To serve him is to serve the world, or so he says.
Gather the best, show that the perfect harvest

is proof of love. Today I walked and walked
until I saw the Edges, where trees bend with fruit

that glow and droop with yearning to be plucked.
There I saw odd gaps between the stalks and leaves,

a sort of emptiness, without the vapours of clouds
even. My own breath against my face felt strange

with this new un-knowing. I walked on, but every
time I approached, the vines closed in. I pushed

deeper, and they wrapped tighter, and crushed
what I couldn't see. Each time I moved further

some winged guard would appear from the fringes,
saying *nothing no   thing to see, nothing at all*

best to go back, love.   Go back to love.

So I will watch him sit, gesture, and speak
with the things I put into his mouth. He will offer

his glorious guest, and they will eat. They will sip
the nectar I decanted over the past hours.

The heaviest blossom are the ones still unopened,
who has time to savour their fragrance?

All flowers resist the prising apart of petals.
Since the cut of my birth, I had to be careful:

a bruise can release such bitter juice. I must do
as he says. Sometimes I wonder if I cut myself

open, spread out my flayed skin, lay the quarters
of my heart before him, will all be pleased?

The box of caulis sat on the ground in the middle, next to the cabbages. Above were rows of fruit, arranged in heaps in their bright colours. A drizzle had started, the kind that melts into the greyness of city and fragments of sky that hung that day over Holborn. The stall was tucked at the head of this alleyway, next to the no. 59 bus stop. I was near the end of the queue, holding a pineapple, *produce of Costa Rica* – its spikes were loosening, readying its ripeness. Someone asked the man for Bramleys, said the cherries looked nice. She was walking by, hunched over, hands in the pockets of a worn velvet jacket – young, perhaps a student, I thought. Her movements were quick, sudden, with the grace of a sea-bird swooping down to the rising shoal. She bent down with a little curtsy, scooped the big cauli into her chest, folded the wings of the jacket over it, cradling as if it were a sleeping newborn, and without a break in the dance, she stepped onto the bus. The doors *shushed* closed after her as if part of the caper. She was settling at the window seat when our eyes met, and though I smiled, and bus was moving off, her face froze. Then the brazenness and joy of her actions lifted off me, soured to thoughts of leaving home, of the sadness of monochrome vegetables.

WHEN SALLY GAVE ME FLOWERS

The day brightened. The office lights weren't on
yet the blooms glowed their own fluorescence,
white upon white through their plastic wrappers,
stretched their patterns onto the meeting table,
silhouetted leaves and stems through the glass worktop,
fracturing as the shapes bent at the edges of chairs'
legs tucked under.
              Three bunches: the type of roses
where the petals gather at the base with green veins,
delicate lace waiting for decay, yet managing to hold all
together. Three: to be divided between work, home
and safe house. From then on, I bought myself flowers,
learned to walk past sullen dogs, to ignore the snarls
and bared teeth, learned to watch the table balance
the droop and lift of unfurling bursts of little joys.

ICE CREAM SPOON IN THE OFFICE
(after Jan Wagner)

This heat should call for it, but we use it to measure sugar
& grounds of coffee. Yesterday I cleaned it with bleach.
Now, inside its shine, the room is cupped until windows
curve at each lip, the fluorescents on the ceiling make
its shadow indistinct on paper printed with words that
ask *write on small things* & yet the heat lingers over this
lunchtime silence, among the tables & chairs – look – even
flies from the bins outside on the pavement come in from
the stink, & flit from desk to desk & go out again. But
soon coffee will summon, & this small thing will return
to the plastic rack, in the little kitchen hidden behind the
archives, back to gauge & stir hot liquids, never to scoop
that cold sweetness, release the drip of melt & shock of
stickiness, the lick of tongues.

COLLEGE REUNION AT THE MERCATO METROPOLITANO
(i.m. Richard Reid)

Jim was on his way back to Zimbabwe from the Belfast wedding. Nick was waiting with a pint of German Kraft beer. Dylan turned us down, said he had to be at a board meeting. Mike said *thank fuck for that!* Glaspole turned up with his wife Jenny – I recalled her making my wedding dress, how she sewed, so precise, hundreds of seed pearls along the satin edges. Tom whispered that the trial drugs really helped his MS. Caroline messaged she was on holiday in Cornwall. Ainslie was still designing old people's homes. He said Liam had collapsed with a brain tumour, died in the ambulance, and Garry was crushed on his bike by a lorry. Bob gave up building glass towers and works from home now. Ron showed his photo collection of footbridges. Dick wept as we still remembered him, wanted him there.

Mouse stays quiet in crowds. He leans against the wall when the class is photographed. The others make startled faces, laugh with open arms. He pulls away in his New Romantic glow, hair tufted and yellow, changes his smoothed fur for corduroy trousers. His little paws are tucked into the pockets, feet dirtied in the same mud as the others. Mouse marks his deafness with insouciance. He likes to play the bass. The low frequencies thump through his belly, and can penetrate brick walls. Mouse's eyes are glacial blue, but will never see a glacier. He doesn't like the idea of retreat. Mouse saw his parents die though their bodies still moved. He grew afraid he would fade to disappearance, as they did. He remembered their grimaces when rugs on the floor became holes to fall into. Mouse tried to carry them when they forgot how to walk. Mouse begins to scramble faster on his wheel. He decides he will not wait anymore. Mouse begins to see freedom every time it rains.

LIMEHOUSE REACH
after Antony Gormley

a man rises
        out of the river
until the horizon forms a line

with his eyes, the rays
        of midsummer
will pass through his arms

as if they were
        sheaves of corn
his skin is rust

he stands over the flood
        where the water
holds the colours of overcast

skies, and moss on ancient timber
        here, the foreshore
coughs up its own riches

a waterman's badge
        pieces of blue china
and glass, polished to cloud

snapped flint pieces among remnants
        of old jetties, still with
cast iron dolphins fixed to breast

or moor with chains and fraying
           rope that once held
barges against their posts

there was even a dying whale
           whose body would be
carried by the ebb, to sink

into the black silt that had
           settled over the centuries
onto its ancestors' bones

OGMORE BY SEA
Glamorgan, Wales

Here, the river widens half a mile before it meets the sea.
At springing tides the currents roll in different shades of silt
and granite grey. I've stood on higher rocks and seen a flow
that hits the ebb with a violence only surf, an unleashed river
and roughened beds beneath can show. There's a battle of
waves that pull and push, yet finally accommodates. But when
the tide is low, and sands stretch out from cliff to shallowness
of sea-shelf, saturated ground becomes a view that shines.
It throws a glow that spreads to all it meets: wet sand and
rock, salt spray, the play of children, walkers' dogs that leap,
the circles of crying seabirds, and the sky itself, that in turn
reflects a new radiance towards us, touching clothes, our hair,
our skin, sharpening our shadows that lengthen as we turn
towards our homes.

ANGUILLA

We saw it from the boat, a patch
of something dark against the concrete
pier below the bridge, something

sinuous with a little snout. The boatman
said it was eating a fish, its shape stood
out against the river's clouds of silt

then it ducked into the flow, to reappear
behind us as we sailed past. It must have
entered this estuary decades ago

on the highest tides, springs in spring when
the swell would've been best for its body,
just a few inches long then, so transparent

it'd be called *glass* before heading upstream
towards fresher water. I began to wonder,
as autumn's equinoctial tides weren't far off,

whether it was ready to return to its birthplace
far out in the ocean, where saltwater shades
of the mid-Atlantic would draw the colour

of sea skies down, through that clear lens
of the depths. Its eyes would grow large, its skin
would smoothen to velvet and turn to silver.

They would gather in their thousands to wait
for some stormy night, when the half moon
begins to wane, and they would set off moving

with the flood and ebb, even slipping over land,
to end in the gigantic gyres of ocean centres,
where sargassum gathers and floats like vast

oil-slicks. They spawn there. But no one has ever
seen these mysteries of suppleness writhing
in the sea. No one yet knows how their larvae,

as tiny leaves in the water, are carried by currents
to coasts and estuaries, where massive ships
crawl with their tugs, to docks that hold the world's

possessions. Our glassy elvers would move
from brackish flows, towards a freshwater home.
With skins darkening to brown and yellow,

they'll glide unseen past the rippled shine
of mud banks, where seals rest, and little boats
of the port sail under the straddle of huge bridges.

It is 33 degrees outside & I am trying to write about eels & a river five thousand miles away. I think about sargassum, so orange and thick floating in the Atlantic, I thought it was a huge oilslick when I first saw it from an airplane window. Eels are born there. It is almost half three in the afternoon, there is no wind to cool the damp heat, & my mother has finally fallen asleep. I had snapped her dose of painkillers into pieces small enough for her to swallow. My sister arrives & we look at film of my mother & aunts who reminisce about their childhoods, & *their* mother's final days. Outside, three parakeets squabble on the wires that stretch across the road.

When my sister leaves, the quiet returns. Perhaps a few words may filter through about seeing that eel from a boat on that river that is five thousand miles away. How black it seemed in the water, how it looped through its own wake. But now, clouds are towering over the Hill in front of me, vapour made to seem solid by the setting sun, fractal edges lit to brilliance on one side, dark & thick on the other. The sky fades to white, & I wait for the sudden nightfall of home. Crickets crescendo, the house gecko slips past, he stops to stare at me and darts up my mother's hanging fern. A stray chicken settles to sleep in the pomegranate tree. She is not afraid of thunderstorms. The Hill turns black, and I go inside.

COLŌNIA

3rd August 1492   Castile
(Columbus set sail)

The world is a larger place than you think. See how the horizon
curves its signal, calls you: *fool.*

12th October 1492   San Salvador
(Columbus makes landfall)

You will erase our name. Say it: *Lucayan.* You will even remove the
name of our land. Say it: *Guanahani.*

25th December 1492   Hispaniola
(Santa Maria runs aground, men left behind to settle)

You ignore the portent of your wrecked ship. The men you left
behind exchanged death for our kindnesses.

MORUGA

south coast, Trinidad

St Peter stands high up with his back to the sea,
arm raised to bless fishermen as they pass to drag
their pirogues along the sand towards the waves.

They will cast their seine into water that lies between
this stretch of island shore, and a mainland where cities
of fools' gold miraged themselves against the greed

of ship-borne adventurers. *May your nets be forever filled.*
The men scaffold and wrap fluorescent tarpaulin with wire
around his body, string light bulbs from the stone hem

of his robe. The wind scours his face with salt and sand,
while vultures circle and settle at his feet. But his gaze
remains unchanged. He marks the spot where three ships

landed over five centuries before, and those greedy
for spice and silk stepped onto this island, conjuring up
the Trinity in its name. They returned to their galleons

to write of lakes of black pitch that spat out forests,
how they sailed through the open mouths of sea serpents
and dragons. Peter's eyes keep their watch, over three

mountain ranges, fallow sugar cane fields, oil refineries,
then on towards a tilted lighthouse set at the other tip
of the island, and beyond that even, over oceans

that hide their boiling chasms, which crush then stretch
to split the earth. He traces the paths of birds that cross
the breadth of the world, follows their songs which

carry him to sail among clouds, each note, each phrase,
precise in its message, weaving, then unravelling
their own nets of call and response, call and farewell.

there used to be whales here, a century and a half ago: finned,
pilot, humpback mothers who hugged the coasts with their calves
       whaling stations lined the Bocas, factories of death that boiled,
skimmed and poured gold oil into barrels
       while inland, the plantations whipped and boiled their own
heat to sweetness

but the whales were hunted until
   there were only dolphins left, with their inedible guile
       too playful and small for serious killing

                              our barrels hold a different oil now
                              black, thick, indelible on the water

       the boats still patrol these waters
hoping to fish more than fish
       night searchlights trained to skim the gaps between breakers
while mothers hold their young up
       to blow, to catch the air against the push of waves

On 24 April 2019, the Jhonnaly Jose, a fishing pirogue, overloaded &
carrying over 33 Venezuelan refugees (mostly women with children) while
crossing the Gulf of Paria to Trinidad, capsized in rough seas. Only 11 were
found alive.

LIMBO

Sea mist has rolled in too quick tonight. He must
be there, on the other side, where the bridge meets
land. Perhaps it's hiding his shape. I remember

that hot day here, so many years ago, he stood
under sea-almond trees, chatting to fisherfolk
while they tended their seine. He'd stopped the car

for me to walk back along the unsteady boards,
to film the stretch and curve of suspended cables,
how their vertical strands swung in slight breezes

yet kept their strength, held tight over the lagoon.
The water was a clearer blue then, deeper than
that day's sky even, beyond the black mangrove

that wrapped around the river's mouth. Pirogues
had moored along the banks, their sides clanked
with red/white/black stripes, names of *Paradiso*

and *La Divina* painted on in untidy letters. Now,
all that remains for us, years later, is that path
across a swaying bridge, lined with wooden boards.

The shadows are causing its rough grain to sharpen,
make the boards turn into drawn lines, spooling out,
faint yet moving, always tracking ahead of our steps.

3 TO 11/ 11 TO 7/ 7 TO 3/ DAY OFF*

I didn't recognise my mother's voice. She woke to find
a man searching the wardrobe. Her hoarse screams had
scared him off, she said he jumped out through the
window. The neighbours joined us, sat to wait in the
porch for police. My siblings handed out Nescafe and
Crix with Anchor cheese, while the elders exchanged
theories of who the culprit could be. I watched the dawn
for the first time. But within days the house was changed.
New swirls of black wrought iron screens would cover
windows. Glass panels in doors were filled with plywood
for strong locks to hold. The gates outside were now kept
shut. Mammy's roses and croton near the tall poinsettia
were cut back, made so sparse, our Alsatian whined for
her usual escape when she caught glimpses of the road.
Then came the night when Mammy turned the lights
on everywhere, scooped me out the bed, held my sleepy
four years as if I were a newborn, sang *doux doux darlin
sugar honey plum plum* while she paced up and down the
living room, for hours, waiting, waiting for Pappy to come
home.

* the shift rotations times for workers in Texaco's Pointe a
Pierre refinery, Trinidad in the 1960s & '70s

YOU WILL OBSERVE...
after Ross Gay

that all his life he had worked
for Texaco, not in the burning field
but as a chemist in the Lab, which means
perhaps he never witnessed the thrill
of a strike. Despite our neighbourhood,
he'd allow anyone into the house
to watch tv (the first in the street). It's likely
some would have stayed, expecting to be fed
as they sat on the floor and continued
to do nothing but stare at the screen.
He taught me Arabic letters as creatures
like treefrogs, that leave wet footprints
as they leap between shade and sunlight,
into leaves of *Aleph, al-Fathiha*, until
alone, he whispered *Ya-sin* with his last breath.

MON REPOS

San Fernando dawn: condensation drips and rolls
against the sounds of barking dogs and slow traffic.

A bluebird with bread in its mouth flies past
the hut where six children live. Among peeling

paint vines spill through open windows of the derelict
house across the street. Pomegranate and rose

bushes shelter below hibiscus trumpets. The stray cat
ignores a butterfly, a flutter of red on black fur.

A dove balances on a telephone pole while
in the distance black shapes of vultures keep circling.

The sky cannot be seen for the clouds. A helicopter
appears from the mist, army green and gunmetal.

Women sit to talk while peeling garlic, laughter mixes
with coffee. *We will cook curried goat for the wake.*

My mother points to birds nesting on the wire, she says
your father's pets. She starts to cry. Eleven o'clock morning:

wasps build a new nest in the house's eaves, cells made
of paper. I am made to pick string beans before the rain.

The air is too still, sweat soaks my shirt. A woman
walks slowly down the Hill, past our porch. She smiles

and stops to talk. She calls her bruise *my daily blessing*.
Noon: not one leaf moves. The clouds thicken

and gather over the Hill. We wait. A drop of rain
hits this leaf then that one. At last the storm has broken.

The phone rings, no one picks it up. Outside, the wind
bends the trees, gutters overflow. Rain thumps

on banana leaves, throwing a mist through the glass
louvres in my bedroom. A bird bathes on an upturned

plant pot, while the tv reporter says she has found
an elderly couple, who sleep among the tombs.

They say *there was no where else to go, and we cannot hide
from the rain*. A Samaritan donates a tin shed but his rent

must still be paid. Days lengthen here too at this time
of year, a whole twenty minutes more. Mosquitoes

emerge from the dusk, to prick constellations
of blood onto my legs. Their high-pitched whines

mix with the drums and candlelight of a distant
congregation's hymns. Darkness falls too quick.

Sandflies loop around street lamps, the stray dogs
group and bark. One stops to howl like a wolf.

Eleven o'clock evening: the scent of jasmine
and sweet lime lingers. Next door's tv light flickers

through their shutters. The street dogs fall quiet.
Midnight's moon will soon rise over the wet rooftops.

His mother chew his ear off. His siblings push him away, so my father friend bring him home in a shoebox. We put him with the guinea pig. The hutch was in the yard, under the rose mango tree, where yard fowl stroll past the stinky duck pond. I feed him hibiscus and roses. Eric thrive. But when we come back after holidays in the Mayaro house, sand still rubbing between my toes, we housesitter uncle say all-you rabbit run away and my father grumble what, run to stew pot eh? Uncle stay quiet. Guinea Pig huddle in the far corner of the hutch, away from the light, refuse to come out for my handful of petals, refuse to eat anything. He fur matt up and one morning before school I find him curl up on he side, open-mouth and stiff. I know from them tv shows that a kiss could make a baby. Eric and Guinea Pig share food then quarrel then play then fall asleep in a tight snuggle over and over. When Pappy put the little body in the shoebox and bury it behind the pond, I see that a boy-rabbit and a boy-guinea pig could love enough, and without each other, even flowers have no meaning.

PARING

this should be about your hands
but I can only think   about a chair   and you

    rocking

as you set the stainless steel bowl
on your lap and lifted your knife   how you cut

your loneliness   in the daytime

with phone calls and shouted greetings
to neighbours   as they pass

while your pet hen   clucked softly
below the porch   the dog would glance at her

then settle down on the steps   both adopted strays
unlikely friends always together   but this should be

about your hands   yet an image of a white orchid
is unfurling above its clay pot   sways

so slight   in the breeze that passes through

the pomegranate tree which bore fruit
to red ripeness only   after you had left

CURFEW

Oh the heat of *petit carême*!
How it loads its weight across our shoulders,

spreads over the cane fields and oil derricks
while some hurricane, a thousand miles north

from these two islands, sucks all the moisture from the air,
but leaves a gift of stillness, over burning skin and breath

that scorches, even under these blanket greens
of pomme cythere, avocado, rose mango, watermelon,

things now in season, rude ripeness bursting out
to take advantage of this little drought

that's tucked between rain, rain that seemed
to never go away, but it did, just for this small

part of September, so even the water in the pipes
was locked down to save itself, just as our lives

are now locked down. Listen! The dogs
have stopped barking, although they'll still

pleasure themselves with soft howls at a waxing moon,
as if they know that gun shots and screams and sirens

will not disturb their masters' sleep, at least
for these few months, when we could pretend
that all is well, and night time is a safe house.

petit carême: tr. 'little Lent' – Creole term for a sudden dry spell in the rainy season of the Caribbean.

For three months in 2011, a State of Emergency was declared in Trinidad & Tobago after a spike in gang-related murders. Anyone caught outside their home between 9 p.m.–5 a.m. could be arrested and fined.

NINE FINGER MILO

I was out in the backyard, outside by you tantie maid room

bent over our fishing poles   no moon that night   we couldn't see his face

that cutlass was sharp, oh gad oh boy!

he could never stop telling his stories   the sea breeze was faint   nothing else moved

man I was cutting them coconut, that young green kind for water, you know?

to my cousins   this story was already old   but not to me

You hold the nut in one hand and whapwhap! Chop the top, then you could drink

new moon under our footbridge lagoon water reflected stars bright as above

but this time I slip, me ain't know how and I did chop me finger off!

the bile rising in my throat   no one was saying stop   we know we know

Ooh gooosh the blood spurt out, and then a chicken come, grab the finger in she beak and run!

my cousins laughed at the punchline   as the sky broke apart   in ripples of my vomit

Come children, climb in them seat. They leather line and warm, but miss out one-two, stay arms length apart before we go start. We go slide past them aisle stack up with tin fish, dry peas and rotten fruit. Let we fly through them wide-open freezer doors, and hold on firm, just for this! Gardez! How we hook and hang up wild meat, swing carcass in we own slipstream breeze. While everything around moving to millennia musak, watch how we dodge and shoot past all that melt and stink. We go slide past monoculture - easy now - we moving on well beyond, breezing through all them colony, one after the other, while they fall bap! bap! and collapse down like domino, into their own kinda disorder. Don't forget to breathe. In. Out. And light plenty torch on the way. We plan good eh? Here, pick up some of this wood: it nice and dry and easy to burn. Now clap and sing out with raise-hand praise:

[full brass band with
kettle drums, crescendo]

> *When you breed a dog to kill, it could only kill!*
> *When them gear get perpetual oil, they go never stand still!*

[decrescendo, with
pandeiro roll]

So keep going little ones. Speed up quick quick. Put on your mask, make sure to breathe from them tank. Filter your water well. You could see? You could count? Bounce babies, bounce. Fly even higher! Watch what we doing and make sure to follow. Mark up we game, because we write them odds. After all, hell done flip over, so who laughing now?

CARNIVAL OF SMALL CREATURES
after Martin Carter

This is the time of masks, little one.
All round the streets, the naked crawl about
their troughs of glitter-dust, until skins reflect the sky.
Red lips of clowns are painted in pretend sorrow.

This is the season of masks, little one.
It is the bacchanalian dance, half-masked with feral tears.
It is the festival of black oil, igniting fires of misery.
Everywhere revelers' debts rise: may they never grow anxious.

Who'll pay to play the Devil's Masque this time?
Whose body will lie among the razor grass?
It is the scent of death, little one, that silent invader
Watching our words and infecting our dream.

WRECKED

dead brothers never leave
they stay to whisper commands
               they laugh   and tease

I'm snorkelling in the clear water
of the cove, though face downward
I know it's you because
             how can water sing?   below us

ribs of an old hull curve up
like the fingers of a giant, half buried
             lying on his back   he watches

while the tide lowers
so when I float past, white
coral sand dislodges
             small darts of fish   they turn scarlet commas

against blackened remains, and you
had said it burned, grew so hot
             even the sharks stayed away   to wait for

those who were free enough
to jump from flames, became
easy meat that night
             moon-less dark   over bodies left below

still tangled among rope and chains
though saltwater disintegrates iron
             the barnacled husk   of submerged wood persists

now my shadow slips
over the sea floor, the noon
sun burns my back
                              as clumps of sargassum   unravel into trails

while you drift between me
and that Atlantic sky

BOUNDARY
after Lisa Brice

it felt like home
but not the usual kind of place
I would frequent

because I am a good girl
even though I want
to call you dilettante

I could still smell the rotting fish
as dirty water pooled
in the cloggup drains

this part of Port of Spain
does climb out of a white coffin
once the streetlights turn on

the doubles and aloo pie
and empanada sellers not even
finish setting up their stalls

now too early even for
cricket crowds to start their
trawl for pavement park

inside I walk around where
you mind-darken a room
with Paramin blue outlines

of diablesse posing as jamette
who touch men with a/c chill
hands to cajole for a Stag

where pink lipstain fluoresce
on green bottleneck to string
the whole night through

red/black/white pvc strip curtains
and lock-in windows laced
with wrought iron fretwork

KAIETEUR FALLS
(Potaro River, Guyana)

'Out of curiosity, our physician on location… wanted to see the
mysterious nesting place of the swifts.
From the bottom of the falls, the gigantic cave is inaccessible…
We lowered a camera to him…
Later, we decided not to show his footage. [due to the wishes
of the local people]'
The White Diamond (2004), Werner Herzog

In that scene, there were swifts that live in a cave
behind a waterfall. At daybreak, they would fly

out through the water, murmur into the shape
of a monstrous grackle, feathers flickering black

iridescence. The dark shape spins and explodes
to a blurred pixilation in our mind's frame.

Again and again they coalesce and split into waves,
unroll as giant arabesques that curve against

the screen of the sky. We are made to hover
over the paper white of the mist. It shimmers

in the sunlight, forms a rainbow at its belly.
The water pours from a point so high, we never

question its power, never look up, and we cannot
see what ends below. In the distance, mountains

fluoresce, clouds pump their heartbeat colours
while through all this, the water continues

its endless spitting. There is nothing else to bear
while that moisture clings to our skin. Sometimes

we can glimpse the cave when the wind gusts
and billows the fall. The sheet lifts, folds, shows us

the open mouth. The sky begins to darken, and they return.
Now their sound becomes a mass that wraps into a point:

watch how they unravel to form a snake of coal dust
that plunges through the fine spray, into the hollows,

until the tail whips across to snap the curtain shut, smooths
white noise of water over the silence of sleeping birds.

WHITE NIGHT
(Jonestown, Guyana)

'but across most it sweeps / As they all might have done had
they been loved.'
Faith Healing, Philip Larkin

I remember as a child seeing the news
of somewhere too close to home.
Hardened reporters couldn't place
the words at first; the cameras swept
across a horror that bloated too quick
in the humid heat. In black and white,
our TV screens showed beyond neat gardens
with lines of fruit trees, too new and young
to bear, and those other rows: some face up,
some down, lying curled to spoon their children.

> *here little one   drink my wine-coloured blood*

The forest had watched it all, and waited.
It knew that those who claimed they'd bless
the spirit, could also break it. The forest beckoned,
held out its own Host to melt on the tongues
of any who had the strength to run to it.

Decades on, visitors say as they walk
among chest high bushes, only silence
no birds, no bugs, nothing

Note:
*'White Night': warning code for crisis defence rehearsals & suicide
drills of Jim Jones' Peoples Temple
'no birds, no bugs, nothing' as noted by journalist Julia Scheeres*

HERETIC
(after Dante, redacted)

      the squall sent
a sound   one that ripped
along the dust   before
making   beasts   run   for shelter

while
      your eyes fix where
      the smoke is thickest

while
a thousand ruined   scatter away
and wait for   some messenger to sign away   **silence!**

what scorn there   is for outcasts

      why do you set   yourselves   against your own rebellion
close   your   open gates   learning nothing
but itch to laugh at those who burn

           while

a city with a river   will still   sink into stagnant marshes
in a country bounded   by a sea   whose waters
   wash   uneven tombs
buried in   a ring   with lids upraised   un-
ending   and between

To what degree? The spit? the snarl? The triumphant shouts of *we voted you OUT OUT OUT!* to bewildered Indian tourists on the Tube that Friday? The neighbourly curse of *you dirty bitch* on the Saturday after, while you are standing in your own garden, touched by the wonder of the first ever apples showing on that gift of a tree - no June drop that year - or maybe where passing on the street is met with narrowed eyes, flared nostrils, the stiffening of bodies, the clutching ever-so-more-tight of handbag as you brush by, the hard-to-define way of being always in the wrong, where only those like you know, this is not *only thoughtlessness* or *I know what you mean.* Only those like you know what this is - this type of - this. The worst of it is the smallest cut. The worst of it is silent.

Watch how the skin peels, dislodges, is sloughed off to reveal inner layers of mottling, so soft and moist. This holds a tint only burning sugar can show, at that instant when it granulates from smooth clay to sheets of beaten copper. This wound, just here on the trunk, has already dried. Even the leaves turn brittle, curl into fingers, and desiccate to crumbs. Examine these differences of duskiness, the scale of halftones that play out among and over us, during our quick dawns and lingering twilights. How many will mingle in crowds, to be tied to others with strings of painted lines? Which of these, when they touch and interweave with us, will you still believe are invisible? Remember, remember the splintering of their scent through the prism of air, the lick of it, the hot taste against the inside of our throats, the hurt on, the hurt of the tongue.

WHEN WE WERE 10, WE SAW A BOY BURST INTO FLAMES

But there were no fire, only spirals of soot that swirled into poinsettias and buttercups.

The billows formed a pitcher-plant shape, swelled to curve into a brim of thundercloud smoke.

A woman on the pavement screamed when something crawled out, still alight. It moved again, became a dog, then a small human shape on all fours.

He raised an arm when the taxi driver ran up to douse the heat with the white ice of an extinguisher.

Then the boy rocked and moaned, collapsed in the foaming patch of road that stank of spilt gasoline.

We children watched, silent, as the men pulled his burning bike away from the crude-black riverbank, and gathered their sorrow around his flaking body.

while playing with my cousins on the asphalt parking lot outside my Uncle's roti restaurant, on the main street in Marabella, south Trinidad. How distanced are our childhood selves to whomever we've become now, when the years ahead are petering out? To live in a refinery town during a time when health & safety laws were not enforced, the possibility of disaster was as an acceptance, as a type of normal. Was this the life around all such industries? where a merging of variables - weather, human error, machine failure, hubristic design - implodes to a point of where catastrophes blossom into disaster. I recall lying on my mother's bed, days after seeing the boy, knowing and understanding what I felt was shock. The adults were carrying on with their lives, unaware of what we children had seen. Then came a clear decision: *stop thinking of this NOW, or else you will never stop seeing it.* And I did, and it worked, until my mind grew strong enough to manage. The child's instinct knows the safety of cold thoughts, the protection of shutting off. How wise we were then.

SANCTUS

(a re-telling of the UNHCR definitions of the displaced)

Someone tells them: wait for a port in a storm, search for bedlam. Each year, more and more people join this pilgrimage. So many of them try their best to shield their longing for the persistent power of a roof.

*

Those who refuse to move, skim the periphery of their own ruin. Even inside, they are still at large, breaking into cradles, wearing down hearths, making nests from their own bedclothes. Often, despite the thorns and knots, they will not shift position. As a result, these are among the most fragile.

*

In your mind's eye, everything fades at the sound of constant rain. If you made love, you may enter into a pact with your lover. If you did not, you would speak plainly, nothing is left broken, even yourself. But beware: you could become closed off, left spellbound by the beauty of bare bones and unshod feet.

*

These people disown the heavens until the stars are no longer distinct. They will not be taught anything new, so do not repair their walls or roofs. Though they cross over your fields, they cannot touch you or what you own, even if you offer it. Yet without these things, their existence has no relief from sorrow.

*

Sometimes they choose to re-enter their chambers, where each hollow fits a particular desire. But be cautious, their wounds might be pulled open. The laments last for years, sometimes without a single tear. They know they are watched, re-measured, for more breath, more bleeding.

*

Their earnings are nothing, yet they show gratitude, and take great care when choosing one object over another. Over the years, they have watched waves rise, swamp fields, dislodge biting beasts. But for now, they stand safe above the swell. Soon they will return, to re-bond their shattered bowls until the cracks glow gold.

LET US MOURN THE DEATH OF KING SUGAR

Note: Production of sugar in Trinidad and Tobago lasted over 300 years. After the enslavement of African people, and Indian indentureship, the industry remained as employment for over 10,000 workers. In January 2003, the now state-owned industry was broken up and shut down suddenly by the government, mainly due to cuts in EU subsidies. Despite protests, the agricultural land was redeveloped including for other uses, including building. The country's physical and emotional landscape is changing after centuries of toil on rolling hills of sugar cane. Never again will miles of white cane arrows waft in the dry season wind. The acrid scent of burning sweetness will no longer hang in the air.

WE CONDEMN YOU

this is a slow dying
                          calluses cover your hand
and two hundred years later
          you still can't feed your children

blackbird and egret call out
over cut cane
but cane
        go always bleed he sweetness
whether you alive or not

so slow down now, slow

they ain't going to need you
so much, soon come

they forgetting you
they forgetting your scent
your soft grains of Demerara gold

them tongue and belly
start to yearn only for that other
cheap
        quick
                kick of white

WE PLACE THE BURDEN ON YOUR SHOULDERS

you learn fast here
dawn does bring long-tail whips
     that crack between corridors
rooms with no windows
     doors lockup from the outside

so put on your *wey fe do*
carry your *hang 'pon me*
and *goudy*
         hold your cutlass close
keep that blade keen

you go cut no more than twenty tonnes
even though your children's
children's children
could cut twenty times more

because for them
     this is work to choose
or not
     to start or
         to walk away
whenever they want

YOU FALL

remember the vessel
that carry the stench of death?

remember the song
that rise to a howl   then drop to a low low moan?

listen:
it come in over the salt spray

this is a tune of too-tight shackles
                        scraping against sores
a jingle   of butcher bracelets and iron necklaces

watch nah   how sharks follow the rhythm of the wake
                            behind the boat
watch how it stretch from one side to the other
across a whole ocean

      smelling blood that leak from a ballast of souls
      smelling blood that soak every grain of timber
      smelling blood that stain them same hands that betray you

we does smell that same stink in your first home

when them ship have sails with belly full of wind
it does roar like wave slamming stone on beach

and if they let you out for air   rope go still tie around your waist
                 cut right through your skin

and that is just the beginning

because you go heart-bleed for so
for every manjack day of your life

YOU SEE YOUR MOTHER

but you not sure
because she could be any woman
and you could be any child

so call out nah, call out to see if she turn around
call she

> *Nancy, Jenny, Cowslip, Rosemary,*
> *Strumpet, Virtue, Psyche, Venus,*
> *Mimba, Molly, Frolic, Ganymede,*
> *Juba, Beneba, Dione, Qua'sheba,*
> *Euclin, Arabia, Genevieve...*

but if she see you and know you
she must stay silent

they call you Koromantyn
because you don't flinch when you take the brand iron

they call you Ebo
because you cry too much when they set dogs on your sister

YOU PASS ON THE BURDEN

you didn't know, at least not at first
how in a land far over the ocean,
where blue sky was uncommon,
some people find the chains
that massa use to shackle you
even the screws he use to rip your thumbs apart
they see a mask of iron that push your jaws
wide wide open for days
(even massa horse never suffer so)

well them people write down
your story, about the shit-filled ships

and the bodies throw overboard

and the catwhip that skin you alive

and the woman taken anytime massa want

and year after year they shout

and year after year nobody listen

they get stories throw back at them
how them people up in the north
          who had to scrape life
          from dead soil against cold sea
how them have it worse off
          because at least you does get sackcloth
          for clothes, and salt fish to eat

but still the shouts went on
even with letters spell out in clay
                    I not a man too?
                    I not your brother?

and little by little, minds start to change
with help from a not-so-secret wallet
          that open out big big for massa and massa alone

but for you, you get nothing
                    except a slow unravelling, piecemeal
just like in your grandfather story
          where the locust did thief from the farmer grainstore:
                    and another locust come and take another grain a corn…and gone!
                    and another locust come and take another grain a corn…and gone!

YOUR SISTER WIPES YOUR TEARS

this land is a sacred thing
all that grow in it, all that live
and walk on it, know

it have a beauty that does stay
even after everything that
get wipe off until nothing left

except dry and crackup earth
the creatures of the forest
will die, the trees cut for horse

donkey and buffalo to graze
before you had to prepare it
with hoe and ashes, to dig

hole by yourself, because
massa own ox more
expensive than you

and when them ratoon shoots
grow to arrow, so that the hills
look like snowfall from massa

country, when the wind change
and blow over saltwater, now
is the time to lay firebrands

on the fields
now   is the time to watch
the burning

YOU FALL (AGAIN)

if massa pull you from your family:
                    you go stay *you*?
if massa rub out your name:
                    who you go be?
if massa cover your faith with a new one:
                              what you go be?

don't fool yourself:
ragged man always carry massa burden

belly go bleed when spear chook it
church bell cause crow to fly
rain fall after poui tree flower

dead man hang like drying clothes
low swinging chariot go never come

at least not here, on this island
so don't catch temptation and try
to look beyond any horizon

put hope out of your mind
or else you might end up all alone

because pride, pride does go before

YOUR DAUGHTERS OF THE FIELDS MEET

nothing go ever change for we
we have it hard now and forever

sunrise to sunset, spell after spell,
breaking we backs
half a night in a house
line up with coppers, fill-up
with fancy-word tasks:

                clarify   *temper*   *skim*

but for we, *boil* means *boil*

we feed and clean your animals
food cook and lay out for you
your linen wash until the lye
burn skin from we hands

you take we body whenever you fancy
like meat to throw away when spoil

something to sell or buy

so watch now, we dip we finger in saltwater
and touch it to the corners of we eyes
while we listen to we own man
when he look outside to point finger
to say:

       all you obscene
       because you use skin colour
       to discriminate and exploit
       a mere physical difference
       I tell you

then with he same breath
he turn to he wife, or child and say:

> *shut up, do what I say*
> *or I go beat de shit out of you*

YOU FALL FOR THE THIRD TIME

eh eh! Gardez nah! more boats sail
over black water, packed with yet more bodies

fooled by new traps set with arkatia promise
that get break even before the ink of your X

or thumbprint get dry
on your contract paper

> *if you come with us, to our lush fields*
> *and streams of clear water*
> *where your house is your own and wages high*
> *light work, you will only be sifting sugar*
> *if you come, we'll pay for your passage to return home!*

this is a generosity that put a new face
on a old bed, inside rotten-wood barrack

with kitchen sink hangup outside
hole-for-window, where sawdust

could never kill off latrine smell
while twelve have to fit to a room

well boy! you get to keep your name
your faith, at least families get
to stay together   small favours eh?

and a curtain as a wall between a floor
lay out with flourbag mattress

look how generous them people is
so generous to repeat every 24 hour

with spells of the past, yet again
lie to trick same old, same old

although this time round you get
fool with cajole instead of coerce

and when they lead you off that ship
line for barges to transfer to quarantine

island, line up for walking along
that rock that look out to mainland

bigger island, your excitement for
a new life turn frighten, because

all you go see is a line of white guards
wearing white uniform and pith helmet

waiting there for youwith guns

so centuries of toil stretch out
behind and ahead from dusk to dawn

same tasks with same cutlass and plough
same planting, same carts pull by bullock

same burning to harvest, same overseer
same whip   same grog to forget

WE SEE YOUR NAKEDNESS

tell them how this does work nah
show   how is the same difference

      because nothing really change so much
except nowadays is metal put to work instead of flesh
instead of cutlass, is combine harvester
               behemoth the Demerara poet call it
      and oui papa! they big for so
      long long blades that slice when
      they twist and turn, nasty looking

but the method is always the same:
cut close to earth, tear skin
and trim to bone
      to bind up every living thing
with ropes of fear
             after all
ain't that is what all rules
      all laws and power to control
does come from?

Say it again: what you is afraid of
               does drive your life on
               like bullock in front of cart

you hear them whispers
behind you back?

you see them trying to hide
they mouth behind they hand?

you know what they say?
        how you going to be worth
less than nothing in no time

how they could get better   for cheaper
they say you too slow, and you waste
your land
        so many acres spread out
and all you could think of
is old time kind of planting
                        – no profit, no profit in that, boy!

they make your sweetness
turn into something too bitter
        you have to taste
a new kind of burden

look: let we give you
something to cover your eyes
cover your ears, your heart

WE WATCH YOU DIE IN FRONT OF US

so where you go
if your house get bulldoze
by soldiers, who can only see
your children in a playground
as a new kind of shooting game?

nowhere is safe
if a man need to starve
himself to skin and bone
just to get listened to

nowhere is safe
if the lives of your family
is forfeit for
just trying to find food
and you have to beg
on your knees to be saved too

WE PLACE YOUR SHROUD OVER YOU, TO WAIT

So soon they go try to break you
yet again, but this time

you have to stay down because
they go roll heavy stones all over you

they go carve your body up
into little pieces, and sell off

each portion, so that one day
ash and concrete will get pour

into your veins, to form
traces that swell into roads

where rainstorms hold themselves back
inside chambers cut into your ground

until one day, they burst out
with a kind of petty-mort release

watch how it flood and wash
all nourishment from inside you

until your skin, your soul, turn
to a desert, a flat nothingness

spread out to the edge of the sea
until it fill up with your floating dead

and after corbeaux pick at and scour
the bodies, they go settle on the seafloor

pile up so high, your bone mountains
go rise from the saltwater, grow up so high

the tops go start to resemble an island
with outlines of three hills, that hang

right there, draw out the horizon as if
they was stone tombs holding white decay

that had settle to cover, to seal away corpses
of them ancient giants that you used to fear

ANCESTRAL CODA

a demolition, where the heart implodes
a re-building
a child's hand that draws a roof over walls
a pencil cross to make windows black out
a dream that moves you, never to arrive
a bedpost and paper prayers, embedded in foundations
a wooden wall attacked by termites
a miniscule chainsaw that cuts through sleep
a manicured garden
a white rose bush tucked under
a pomegranate tree, where a pet chicken roosts
an overgrown garden
an ex-garden where cars park
a scrapbook of photos and boxes of shells
a lost ticket to a play about a family in a living room
a book where text is so dense the words disappear
a voice that speaks over other voices
a stoppage of kisses
a meal cooked with care that is devoured
a meal cooked with care that is spat out
a flight over black water
a looking down onto the sea
an imagination of whales swimming
a looking down the nose
a change of name, a keepsake of name
a reveal of DNA: of Uttar Pradesh, of Persia, of China, of Micronesia
a legacy of damaged blood cells, with its burden of breathlessness
a halt in the bloodline, a carrying of grief for ghost children
a carrying of their conversations
with you, your parents, their parents

My pen tracks the desire paths of Xinjiang, traces the foothills of the Himalayas, walks 200 miles along a railway line of Empire to Kolkata, sails over kalapani, gives birth in a quarantine ward on Nelson Island, cuts cane for decades, abandons its children, sacrifices for its children, steers Dolly the horse in a hackney cab around 1920's San Fernando, makes black cake at Christmas, makes crab callaloo and sada roti, makes yam and fried plantain, works 40 years in the oil refinery, breathes in sulphur dioxide laden air until street children choke while they play, drives the family to a beach house, watches as oil rigs make a permanent dawn along the night's sea-horizon, grows orchids, sits for 15 years in a wheelchair, waits each morning for hummingbirds in the garden. My pen writes for 7 generations in a country whose keyboards now type: this is not *your* time, it is *ours*. My pen lifts and drips. The ink blots, begins to bleed into other lines. Nothing can be read as the black ink splits and spreads into its chromatogram of component colours. This book is over-used. The spine is breaking. The paper was made the old way. Now the edges of its pages tear up. Is it too fragile to touch? My pen hesitates, wants to pretend it understands, pretend it knows where and when to place its mark.

'I GO SEND FOR YOU'

Rasheedan   *Boodhanie*

My family refused him, said his skin
was too dark. He built them a palace.

          My husband once saw a mongoose battle
          a snake while cane stalks were being set alight.

One night he came to my window.
I wrapped jasmine sheets with dowry gold.

          He led the way for me through the fields.
          The mongoose bit the snake, then smoke covered them.

I walked with him along two hundred miles
of railway tracks, from the mountains to the sea.

          I raised my cutlass each half year, bent my back
          to plant ratoons, before the dry season ended.

The child in my belly bucked more
than the ship that sailed over black water.

          My arms grew strong, my skin turned
          a midnight sheen. My hair thinned to white.

My son was born four days after my feet touched
the stone outcrop of that island.

He collected my 16 cents a day wage, held on to his 25,
said he saved it for us to go back over the water.

My husband could read, they made him a driver of gangs.
I never worked in the fields, the sun hurt my eyes.

When our ten years were done, he put the coins
in a brass lota, wrapped it in a cotton dhoti.

My skin stayed smooth. My sons carried books
to school, their sons taught the sons of others.

He sailed back home with all we possessed, alone.
Each night, I would tell my daughters of his promise.

My youngest brother had followed, refused to sign
any bond, paid his way to look for me.

He would build us a palace, with a garden of
pomegranate trees, and a fountain scented with jasmine.

Ten years later my brother found me, I held him while he cried,
curled in my lap like the baby I remembered.

Each half-year season, I waited for the rain to break
the noonday heat. Every morning, I sharpened my blade.

*My paternal great-grandmother Rasheedan left her wealthy family
in Azamgarh, Uttar Pradesh, to elope with a married man, Ashraf, in
1901. My great-great grandmother Boodhanie arrived in Trinidad
(c.1860). She was abandoned at the end of the contract by her husband
who returned to India, and left to bring up her 3 young daughters alone.*

PARTITIONS
i.m Rasheedan Khan

'...we are all connected by water, la sangre de vida' – Emmy Pérez

My grandmother's mother told her daughters:
do not cry because
I want to go back to India and if you cry I will not be
able to cross saltwater back
but they cried and cried so
did this mean her soul is trapped in
here in the Caribbean? She fell in love with
a married man, he fell for the trickery of arkatias who
promised light work, giving *wonderful accounts of
the place.* She walked 200 miles though
pregnant, with her lover, following
railway tracks, all the way down to
the port. They sailed for three and a half months over
kalapani, and when the ship offloaded onto
barges, the weakened passengers were taken to
that quarantine island, rounded up by
white men in white uniforms and
white pith helmets, colony guards who
pointed their guns at the terrified. Just
off the landing point was the hospital. There were
rooms to die here, yet 4 days after
she gave birth to her firstborn. Today, beyond
that rocky promontory, and among
those ruins, only the lime mortar steps remain. But
there still are more traces left along
the ground, stumps of walls, tiles spread out
on floors of what were once wards, or
morgue. There would have been windows to look out

but by then, she would have been tired of
views of the sea. And when
she breathed her last, over
70 years later, her daughters keening around
her, which India did she pine for?
If her daughters' tears left her soul to
linger between then and now, perhaps
they spared her seeing her country torn apart by
that terrible Midnight of
Partition. And if
her soul knows that if she had held tight onto
the weight of duty, and stayed, then
her whispered *alhumdulillahs* would have led to
nothing but a solitary end, forced to
watch her father's Mughal estate disintegrate, fall into
the river, and left to fade towards
erasure.

GOLD

Think of the girl child, not yet weaned,
and too sleepy to be aware

of the village's women who gather
in the room. Each figure remains

silent. One by one they approach
the cot to slip small gifts under

the sheet: nath, drop earrings, bracelets
stamped with flowers that curve and twine,

chain-linked anklets strung with jet beads
to ward off the evil eye. No

silver is passed, for nothing should
tarnish the baby's future. Now

think of her mother who reaps this
harvest to fill a small basket,

hides this in turn, in her urni
box. She knows that those who are owned,

need to own something of themselves,
even if it must always stay

unseen, unworn, under the lid
of a basket. But she herself

has nothing to give, except her
labour in the fields, with its glint

of cutlass against sugar cane
stalks. Think of the girl, now grown, who

takes hold of the box, unwraps each
veil. Think of *her* daughter's daughter,

who holds your hand, so small in her
palm. She is tying a bangle

around your wrist, pulls so tight,
metal marks your skin, and stays fixed.

MY GREAT GREAT-GRANDMOTHER CALLS TO ME
i.m. Boodhanie Meah

That night after he gone, I lie down, look up
at the ceiling. I hear the people
next door moving in the dark. The baby across

my belly, the girls curl up around me, all I could
think, what else could I think?
except keep the girls safe. Make sure they get a roof

to keep rain and hot sun out, make sure they have
food. What else could I do? except
wake up before day-clean, cut cane   cut

until my *jahaji bahin* step in. Sisters of the ship,
women of these same barracks
come to help feed we, hold baby while I hold

cutlass to cut cane, pile it high on ox-cart.
No cart come for him. He pack
he things in a bundle, and walk away.

Up to years after I would say to anybody
who come from outside the estate:
he name Bachu Meah! They would shake their head,

look away. But my ship sisters help me get roof
over my daughters, find good
husbands who treat them like maharanis.

The middle one, Miriam, married a nice
jahaji bhai son with cat eyes.
Look at your brother sons: same eyes,

same as yours when you was a baby. After my own
daughters, I see all you following-
only a set of girls, or only boys, getting born.

So watch out for when the next set of girls
come. Keep them safe.
Make sure they stand straight-back and look up

at more than ceiling, that they hands cut more
than cane. Make sure they wrap
their own *jahaji bahin* circle tight around them.

* *jahaji bahin/jahaji bhai*- tr. 'sisters/brothers of the ship'
– lifelong friendships & loyalties of indentured labourers,
begun during the voyage from India to the Caribbean cane
plantations (after the abolition of slavery).

BOY

You broke the rhythm of the house,
even though years after, like the years

before, there'd still be the hurried
calls to midwife, water being

boiled, bloodstained sheets for washerwoman
to collect. But with you there was nothing

but silence. Nothing but footsteps
on stairs and the rustle of blankets

being wrapped around my grandmother, whose
eyes were closed, like yours. Exhausted,

she lay unmoving too. You would be
washed, your mouth opened, tongue pressed perhaps for

you to catch some gasp of air. No
one will tell us what sound you made when

the azaan was whispered into your ear.
We do not know when your breath stopped,

if your mother touched the shroud around
your little body. It is said you were

buried in the family plot
where the immortelle trees, so tall now,

with flowers aflame, became the boundary
of the pious and the estranged.

There are no tombstones here, but what need
is there of markers for those without a name?

...but that was not true. They were not our words but we remained quiet. Someone unknown had changed the funeral notice *corrected it* meant well perhaps, or felt a need to cover over this brazen impiety of grief. My mother had refused to move to another place, when the illness left her bedbound – *I not leaving the garden*–even when the only view out was the shut windows of next door. Visitors turned up to pray, chat, entertain or seek horticultural advice. Some bickered amongst themselves, about which plant from her famed collection would be theirs. Once, she wept while telling me about the man who wanted the flowering Cattleya she kept on the little table next to her. She had offered him a different one from the shed outside, potted but dormant, & he walked out angry – *he bawl out, lady take your damn orchid to your grave!* The Cedros Bee specimen, no longer found wild in the island's forests, was her pride. None had noticed it at the side of the house, too small in its pot, too modest, too ordinary looking.

Her haji brothers had her catafalque of woven bamboo laid out in the large hall behind the mosque, with face framed in the white satin hijab & robes she chose, but never wore alive. Her sisters stood in a group, backs towards us, speaking that silent language only sisters know. Then the other women walked in: distant cousins, school friends, from the retirees club, those she chatted to in the grocery, the fishmarket, little shop owners, old neighbours from other towns–& each brought something from their own gardens. One by one, each stepped up to the body to lay their bunch, or sprig, or single flower until, under the circling fans, she was covered in blooms: waxy anthuriums, scented tuberoses like her wedding bouquet, roses, ginger lilies, iris, sharp gladioli, & most of all were the orchids, arranged at the top of the delicate mound, blushed, moist & quivering.

I was the coward. The others were calm. They knew what they had to do. Our cousin Zen was there, she had done this before. Zen is a happy person. She made us giggle in the waiting room, while the funeral director was telling us everybody have a sense they will pass about say maybe 40 days before. Even if they go by accident, he said, and if you see somebody talking to the dead like normal, then you know it ain't going to be long now. Our mother had lain on her sickbed, calling out for us to open the gate for my uncle and them to come in. They outside waiting by the gate, she cried, they in traffic jam, they need to free up. That uncle had died 20 years before. Zen said to the funeral man, eh heh? well that is a nice and cheerful thought!

We had to walk past the showroom – elaborate decorated trays to choose one from, the man said, as muslims don't need coffins, only rattan baskets to degrade quick, dust to dust and thing. He was kind, in his way. Used to the need for speed of these burials. A lady led us into the washing room for the ritual to start. She went into the walk-in fridge and pulled Mammy out on a trolley, wrapped in her bedsheet. oh gorsh she stiff, big sister said, it don't look like she. The lady talked us through the stages, how to wash, how to keep the parts covered to preserve modesty. What prayers to say. She handed out new rubber gloves and showed us the hose spray head.

Middle sister unwrapped the bedsheet from Mammy slow and careful and then we all didn't, couldn't move. Then youngest sister steups and said, all you stop this stupidness ok this is not her ok this is just a shell. She snapped on the gloves and held her hands up like a surgeon and said let's get to work. Brisk

brisk just like so. And then and there we saw the 15 years of her A&E nursing, the calm assessment of disaster with its triage of the distraught, not the images of our forever youngest etched in our minds, the toddler dancing in nappies, or hearing the teenager arguing in the porch with Mammy who would be sobbing: don't ever say I don't love you, you the last one, you go always be my baby!

ACKNOWLEDGEMENTS

Versions of the following poems have been published in:
Mahogany, Traverse, Stonewood Press
Limehouse Reach, Anguilla, Must write about Eels, commissioned poems with the Poetry School & Port of London Authority in response to Antony Gormley's Another Time installation in Limehouse. Published in "Dark Flow: Six Poets responses to the Working Thames" Anthology, ed. Anna Robinson, Thamesis Publications (2013)
Anguilla also published in The Creel Anthology, Guillemot Press (2019)
Delphinus, Heavenly Creatures Anthology, ed. Rebecca Bilkau, Beautiful Dragons (2014)
Cinnamon, Heretic, Filigree: Contemporary Black British Poetry, ed. Nii Ayikwei Parkes, Peepal Tree Press (2018)
Eve Prepares the meal, Poetry School online anthology on Paradise Lost, Simon Barraclough's class on Milton (2017)
Kaieteur Falls, shortlisted entry Montreal Poetry Prize (2017)
Moruga, Mon Repos, The North, Spring Issue 2014
Limbo, Magma 75 "Loss" issue 2019
You will Observe, Paring, Poetry Review, Winter issue 2018
Boy, Brittle Star Issue 36 (2017)
Gold, My Dear Watson, Elemental Poetry, ed Rebecca Bilkau, Beautiful Dragons Press (2015)
I go send for you, We Mark your Memory: Writings from the descendants of Indenture, ed
David Dabydeen, Maria del Pilar Kaladeen, Tina Ramnarine, UoL Press (2018)
Tantie Diablesse Mourns the Death of King Sugar (extract), MPT "Profound Pyromania, 2018 Issue 1.
Washing the body, Partitions, 3 to 11/11 to 7/7 to 3/day off, Poetry Review, Autumn issue 2020

Gulf Of Paria, Wasafiri Issue 109, 2022
Boundary, No flowers by request... Stand Magazine, Winter Issue 2021
Eric, 2nd Prize winner National Poetry Competition 2024